Meditations With

TERESA
OF AVILA

Preface
and Versions by
Camille Anne Campbell,
O. Carm.

BEAR & COMPANY
SANTA FE, NEW MEXICO

Contents

Publisher's Note:

Bear & Company is publishing this series of creation-centered mystic/prophets to bring to the attention and prayer of peoples today the power and energy of the holistic mystics of the western tradition. One reason western culture succumbs to boredom and to violence is that we are not being challenged by our religious traditions to be all we can be. This is also the reason that many sincere spiritual seekers go East for their mysticism—because the West is itself out of touch with its deepest spiritual guides. The format Bear & Company has chosen in which to present these holistic mystic/prophets is deliberate: We do not feel that more academically-styled books on our mystics is what every-day believers need. Rather, we wish to get the mystics of personal and social transformation off our dusty shelves and into the hearts and minds and bodies of our people. To do this we choose a format that is ideal for meditation, for imaging, for sharing in groups and in prayer occasions. We rely on primary sources for the texts but we let the author's words and images flow from her or his inner structure to our deep inner selves.

Preface and Acknowledgments

The great mystics and artists who went before us faced human struggle, suffering, and pain, as we do. They were hungry and thirsty, and , like us, needed the earth for survival. Their tears were salty, their brows perspired, their hearts throbbed as ours. They were oppressed, but continued on the spiraling paths of creation-centered spirituality. They left a rich heritage, but they themselves have been lost over the ages. The controllers of wealth and power have made them into an elite, other-worldly group because they give birth to souls, to the energy needed to transform the world. Such transformation endangers the system which limits human freedom and love.

The truth is that the mystics and artists live most at home in this world, in love with Creator and creation, releasing the energy of compassion so that it flows through all persons regardless of age, race, or sex. They invite us to become the mystics and artists we are capable of becoming, to commune with the universe and the Creator.

We, too, yearn to free the child within, to follow Jesus' warning that, "Unless you become like a little child you shall not enter the kingdom of heaven." A child can be captivated by the wonders of creation: dew on the grass, birds, sky, trees, flowers, and storms. The child is an artist exploring, making things, drawing pictures, inviting "grown-ups" to see through a child's eyes. We yearn to free the artist, the mystic within our hearts, and so expand our souls.

Yet we fear the artist and mystic in ourselves. We excuse ourselves by claiming that we live in a world different from that of John of the Cross, Teresa, Hildegard, Mechtild, Julian of Norwich, and Eckhart. Yet we have the same desires and feelings, share their faith, hope, and love. We must also carry the same cross.

We have, to a great extent, lost our souls. When one has lost the soul, there is no power to be life giving, only the power to destroy. Many people grasp greedily for a greater share of the Creator's gifts than they will ever need in a lifetime. We have nuclear weapons enough to destroy our planet. We live with racism, ageism, and sexism. We cannot give birth to the new age of peace, justice, and love until we recreate our souls, freeing the artist and mystic within.

Who will teach us to give birth to our souls, to be life-giving, creative centers of energy instead of death-dealing centers of inertia? As in every age, God's presence and power will be made known to us, and ordinary people will hear the word of God and act upon it. These ordinary people become known as mystics, described by others as special friends of God who live life fully, recognize the gifts of the Creator, and know how to give birth. They know, too, how to let go and let be, to break through despair and emptiness to release compassion and justice in the world. Mystics are engaged in the process, the transformation and divinization of life, calling us to journey through this exciting experience. To know them is to know the mystic and artist within our own hearts, to accept the challenge to become what God calls us to be.

The *Meditations With*™ series offers us words, images, and experiences that open our hearts to reality. The ancient biblical tradition of creation spirituality frees us from dualistic categories of thought, feeling, loving, and praying which create permanent barriers between God and human, body and soul, male and female, young and old, sin and goodness. Creation spirituality breaks down these barriers with a dialectical dance of love, and Jesus frees us from all dualisms. Jesus is God and man, not an either/or dualism but a both/and act of supreme love. The energy available to the non-dualistic life is omnipresent and inexhaustible.

This, then, is the challenge of Teresa's *Come Out of Your Cocoon:* to search for God in the most deeply personal way; to read the signs of the times in one's own life; to travel the paths of creation-centered spirituality to the center of one's own soul; and to recycle this energy in compassionate loving service. The challenge is not merely to travel back into history, but to march into the future nourished by an inner life of prayer and a hunger for peace, justice, and love for all people and all creation.

Teresa of Avila, born into a prominent family in 16th-century Spain, entered a contemplative Carmelite convent and found that much of her life could continue as before. She had her own private quarters, a parlor for visits from friends, and the routine of religious life. Teresa found that, in order to be true to her vision of the religious life, she had to reform the Order of Carmel. She then led the reformation of her order in spite of illness and opposition.

We all know and live with oppression. The politics, economics, culture, and Church of Teresa's day mirror those of our own, manifesting their various oppressions in similar ways. Oppression is as much a trademark of our mystical brothers and sisters as it is of every person today. Teresa, too, lived with oppression, and wrote of the journey to the center of the castle, the soul, in the midst of it. She was not confined or closed off from the world, but was active in its transformation.

Teresa's reform of the Order of Carmel was a response to the oppression of the Spirit, the result of living an unexamined life. Oppression results when one segment of society determines the role, the function, the way of life of another. In Teresa's case, the Calced tried to define and limit the discalced to which she belonged. Teresa did not hesitate to write to Phillip II of Spain to plead her cause. Monarchs had great influence in the Church of Teresa's day.

An understanding of oppression is essential to an understanding of today's Church, for ours is a church which not only seeks to minister to those oppressed by other social forces, but which must also seek to minister to the oppressed among our own. Our Church is, like Teresa's, a church of sinners seeking forgiveness, a church of confusion seeking enlightenment, of conflict seeking reconciliation. Our Church exists in the world, and has not been exempted by God from the troubles of its time. We must become not a church of men, but a church of the people of God, both men and women. We must own our own story, accept it with love, integrate it into the church we are today, and validate it by our personal, prayerful presence. This is the way of Teresa.

There are six stages in the experience of oppression. We can see these stages in the life of Teresa. The first stage is that of ignorance: The 130 nuns at Avila lived with little awareness of the oppression of the Spirit—and their own spirit—in a time in which women were victims of frivolity, class distinctions, parlor gossip, and minimal prayer time.

In the second stage of oppression, denial, the reality of oppression dawns upon some members of the group, who then disturb other members. Teresa realized the need for reform and was greatly resented: "Who does she think she is? Things are fine as they are. She's just causing trouble. There's nothing wrong with the way we live." There then comes to others some experience which reveals their oppression, and the next stage follows.

The third stage, that of reaction to the awareness of oppression, is rage. This rage is fed by the realization that one's gifts will not be used, that it is possible to function only with the permission of men who undervalue you. Teresa knew this; she sought to use men to struggle with other men in order to gain the freedom necessary to allow the Spirit of God to move in her monasteries. Her letters to the king, to the bishops, and her visits with them reveal the positive way she used the energy of her rage.

Rage changes form and the fourth stage finds one selling out to the oppressor, seeking the oppressor's powers, privileges, and rights. Teresa sought her own visitors, named confessors for the sisters, established her own rule for her convents, but realized the necessity of the bond with the Church and its approval. There is a trap at this stage. Had she continued to identify with the oppressor, Teresa could easily have died a renegade rather than a daughter of the Church. She had the humility and wisdom to seek unity.

Separation from the oppressor marks the fifth stage. As Teresa more carefully identified the oppressor, she sought separate identities for calced and discalced, living to see the distinction established by papal decree in 1580. Her correspondence with Phillip II of Spain brought the rewards, but only after much physical, emotional, and spiritual suffering. Indeed, she had heard the words of excommunication recited to her and the sisters who had voted her prioress.

The final stage, that of the reintegration of oppressed and oppressor as true equals, follows after much suffering, soul searching, and thought. Both groups can and must exist; there is no longer control of one by the other.

Teresa reached the point of reconciliation in her journey through life. The story of her journey inward and then her thrust outward in compassionate love, was written during her struggle with oppression. *The Book of the Mansions* (or *Interior Castle*) describes her journey to the center, where the King dwells, and describes her resultant life of compassionate service.

When I began this book, I gathered Teresa's wisdom from all her works. My cross-referencing revealed consistent wisdom in her works on humility, Jesus, prayer, suffering, extraordinary experiences in prayer, the Jewels from the Creator, the creation-centered approach to life—and throughout was her wonderful sense of humor. As I sifted through the many quotes, however, I realized that to destroy the unity of *Interior Castle* would fail to render the map of the inner journey for today's reader. Although we all travel the same territory, we must each cut our own path. Teresa has given us the guidance necessary to reach union with the Lord, to do what we can to establish peace and justice in our own time. She challenges us to find our souls.

I thank those who have helped me in my own journey and who encouraged me to present Teresa through creation-centered eyes. Matthew Fox, director of the Institute in Culture and Creation Spirituality and my thesis advisor on creation-centered spirituality in Teresa of Avila and John of the Cross, challenged me to do a book for the *Meditations With*™ series. The request was that I use all of Teresa's works. My mother, Mrs. Elise Hughey, read and corrected my notes. My friend and secretary, Beth Ann Simno, diligently typed, corrected, and retyped my manuscript and gave me a lay person's view of the meaning of the journey described by Teresa. Finally, I thank the Carmelite sisters of my congregation who diligently seek to love and serve the Lord.

Path I: Entering In, Listening, Discovering

"Turn your eyes toward the center which is the room or royal chamber where the King stays."

THE SOUL

We are incomparably stupid when we do not
strive to know who we are, but limit
ourselves to considering only roughly
        these bodies.

We have heard and, because faith tells us
        that we have souls,
                we know.

    But seldom do we consider the precious
            things that can be found
                in this soul
                    or
                who dwells in it
                    or
                its high value.

Consequently, little effort is made to
        preserve its beauty.

    All our attention is taken up with the
        plainness of the diamond's setting
                    or
            the outer walls of the castle;
                that is,
            with these bodies of ours.

CASTLE

We consider our very souls to be like a
castle made out of a diamond
or
of very clear-cut crystal
in which there are many dwelling places.

We realize that the soul of the just
person is nothing else but a
paradise where the Lord finds
delight.

The castle has many dwelling places:
some up above,
others down below,
others to the side;
and in the center and middle are the
dwelling places where the very
sweet exchanges of love
between God and the soul
take place.

The door of entry to this castle is
prayer and reflection.

BEGINNINGS

We are speaking to souls
    that, in the end,
        enter the castle.

Even though they are very involved
    in the world,
        have good desires
            and sometimes

        entrust themselves to the Lord
        and reflect on who they are,
            they hurry through it.

During the period of a month they will
    sometimes pray,
        but their minds are
    filled with business matters that
    ordinarily occupy them.

They are so attached to these things
that where their treasure lies,
    their hearts go also.

Sometimes they do put all
　　these things aside,
　　　　and self-knowledge
　　　　　　and awareness come.

They know they are not proceeding
　　correctly in order to get to the
　　　　door of the castle.

Finally they enter the first lower rooms.

But so many reptiles enter with them
　　that they are prevented from
　　　　seeing the beauty of the castle
　　　　　　and from calming down.
　　They have done quite a bit
　　　　just by having entered.

PRESERVING THE BEAUTY

It should be kept in mind here
    that this shining fount,
the shining sun that is in the
    center of the soul,
        does not lose its
            beauty and splendor.

For just as the streams that form
    a crystal fount are also clear,
        the works of a soul in grace
        are most pleasing in the eyes of both
            God and humankind
        because they flow from the fount of life
            in which the soul
            is planted like a tree.

There would be no freshness,
        no fruit if it were not for
            this fount sustaining the tree,
        preventing it from drying up
            and causing it to
                produce good fruit.

DWELLING PLACES ALL AROUND

You mustn't think of these dwelling places
in such a way that one
follows in file after the other, but
turn your eyes toward the center
    which is the room or
        royal chamber
        where the King stays.

The soul is capable of much more
        than we can imagine.

The sun that is in the royal chamber
        shines in all parts.

It is very important
    for any soul
        that practices prayer,
            whether little or much,
    not to hold itself back and
        stay in one corner.

Let it walk
through these dwelling places,
    which are up above,
        down below,
            and to the sides.

God has given it such great dignity.

HONEY BEE OF HUMILITY

Don't force yourself to stay so long in
    one room alone.

Oh, but if it is in the room of
        self-knowledge!

How necessary this room is even for those
    whom the Lord has brought into the
    very dwelling places where he abides.

For
    however exalted the soul may be,
    never is anything else more fitting
        than self-knowledge;
nor could it be,
    even were the soul to so desire.

Like the bee making honey in the beehive,
humility is always at work.
Without it,
everything goes wrong.

But let's remember that the bee doesn't
fail to leave the beehive
and fly about gathering nectar
from the flowers.

So it is with the soul
in the room of self-knowledge.
Let it believe me and fly sometimes to
ponder the grandeur and the
majesty of its God
and the wonders of creation.

THE CALL

This stage pertains to those who have
    already begun to practice prayer
    and have understood how important
    it is not to stay in the
        first dwelling place.

The Lord desires intensely that we
    love him
        and seek his company.
        So much so that
            from time to time
    he calls us to draw near to him.

The call comes through words spoken by
    other good people,
        or through sermons,
            or through what is read in books,
                or through the many things that are
                heard and by which God calls,
        or by illnesses and trials,
            or in enjoying the beauty of creation,
            or also through a truth that he teaches
            during the brief moments
        we spend in prayer.

However lukewarm these moments may be,
God esteems them highly.

DISCOVER A TRUE FRIEND

Reason, for its part, shows the soul that
    it is mistaken in thinking that
      these things of the world
        are not worth anything
when compared to what it is aiming for.

Faith, however, teaches it
    where to find fulfillment.

The memory shows where
    all these things end.

The will is inclined to love
    after seeing such countless signs
        of love;
it would want to repay something;
it especially keeps in mind how this
    true lover never leaves it,
      accompanying it and giving it
      life and being.

Then the intellect
    helps it to realize
    that it couldn't find a better friend,
even if it were to live for many years.

TROUBLES

If you should at times fall,
    don't become discouraged
        and stop striving to advance.
For even from this fall,
        God will draw out good.

Even though we may not find someone
    to teach us, the Lord will guide
        everything for our benefit,
        provided that we don't give up.

There is no other remedy for this
    evil of giving up prayer than to
        begin again;
otherwise the soul will gradually
    lose more each day, and, please God,
        it will understand this fact.

The door of entry to this castle
        is prayer.

Well, now it is foolish to think that
    we will enter heaven without entering
        into ourselves,
        coming to know our weakness
            and what we owe God,
    and begging for God's mercy.

DISCOVERY OF THE SELF:
BEYOND THE EGO

Let me tell you about those
   who have entered the
      third dwelling place,
For the Lord has done them no small favor
   but a very great one
      in letting them get through these
         first difficulties.

I believe that
   through the goodness of God there are
   many of these souls in the world.
They long not to offend God,
   even guarding themselves against
      venial sins;
They are fond of doing penance
   and setting aside periods for
      recollection;
They spend their time well,
   practicing works of charity toward
   their neighbor, and are very balanced
   in their use of speech, in dress,
   and in governing their households,
      those who have them.

Enter, enter the interior rooms
      pass on from your little works.

WELL·ORDERED LIVING—
EGO ACCOMPLISHMENTS

Let us speak now of those souls
    whose lives are so well ordered.
Let us recognize what they do for God,
    and we shall at once see how
    we have no reason for complaining
        against God.

Like the rich young man in the gospel,
    if we turn our backs and go away sad
    when the Lord tells us what we
    must do to be perfect,
    What do you want God to do?
For God must give the reward in conformity
    with the love we have for God.

        And this love must not be fabricated
        in our imagination,
        but proved by our deeds.

        So that we may know ourselves,
        test us, Lord, for you know the truth.

DISTURBANCES: LOSS OF WEALTH

A rich person
    without children or anyone
    who might want her possessions
    might lose her wealth,
    but not to such an extent that
    she lacks necessities
    for herself
        and for the management
        of her household.
    She even has a surplus.

If she should go about us worried
    and disturbed as she would be
when not even a piece of bread were left,
how can our Lord ask her
        to leave all for him.

DISTURBANCES: LOSS OF HONOR

There is a similar occurrence
    when an opportunity presents itself
        for those persons
      to be despised
    or to lose a little honor.

God often grants them the favor
    of enduring such a thing,
      because they have served God well,
for this Beloved of ours is very good.

But now they are left in such disquiet
    that they cannot help themselves,
    nor can they quickly get rid of
        this disturbance.

Aren't these the ones who, for a
    long while now, have considered
    how the Lord suffered and
    how good suffering is and
    who have desired it?

They would like everyone to live
    a life as well-ordered as they do;
        and, please God,
they will not think their grief
    is for the faults of others
      and in their minds
        turn it into something
        meritorious.

DISTURBANCES: LACK OF HUMILITY

If we indeed have humility,
  humility is the ointment for our wounds.

Even though there may be
    a time of delay,
        the Surgeon, who is our Lord,
          will come to heal us.

        Love has not yet reached the point
            of overwhelming reason.

Let us abandon our reason
    and our fears
        into the Lord's hands.

          Undertake with great humility
            the journey I am speaking of.

If humility is lacking,
  we will remain here our whole lives.
If souls are humble,
  they will give thanks.
If there is some lack of humility,
  they will feel an inner distaste
  for which they will find no reason.

For perfection as well as its reward
    does not consist in spiritual delights,
        but in greater love,
            and in deeds done
          with greater justice and truth.

PROJECTIONS

Let us look at our faults
    and leave aside the faults of others;
for it is very characteristic of persons
    with such well-ordered lives
    to be shocked by everything.

Even though we may surpass someone
        in external composure
        and in our way of dealing with others,
            perhaps we could truly learn
                from the one who shocks us
                what is most important.

Although good,
    these latter things are not
        what is most important;
nor is there any reason to desire
    that everyone follow at once
        our own path,
or to set about teaching the way of
    the Spirit
            to people who perhaps don't know
            what such a thing is.

Path II: Expansion

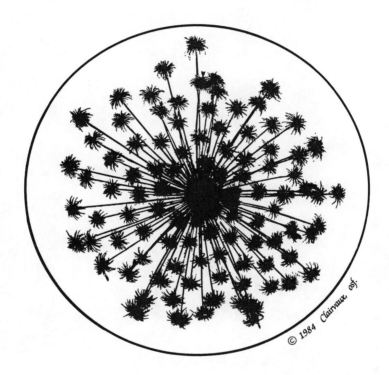

". . . the water comes from its own source, God . . . He
produces this delight within the greatest peace and quiet and
sweetness in the very interior part of ourselves."

JOY

The term *consolations* can be given
    to those experiences we, ourselves,
    acquire through our own
    meditations and petitions to the Lord—
    those that proceed from our own nature.

These consolations arise
    from the virtuous work itself we perform,
    and it seems that we have earned them
        through our own effort
          and are rightly consoled
    for having engaged in such deeds.

But if we reflect on this,
    we see that we experience the same
    joyful consolations in many of the
    things that can happen to us on earth:
        when someone suddenly inherits a
          great fortune,
        when we suddenly see a person we
          love very much,
        when we succeed in a large and
          important business matter
    and of which all will speak well,
        when you see your husband or son
          or brother alive after someone
          has told you he is dead.

Joyful consolations in prayer
    have their beginning in
        our own human nature
        and end in God.

MEDITATION

For the most part,
    souls who have begun the inner journey
    are the ones who have
    these devout feelings,
        for these souls work almost
        continually with the intellect,
        engaging in discursive
        thought and meditation.
And they do well because
    nothing further has been given them,
    although they would be right
    if they engaged for a while
    in making acts of love,
        praising God,
            rejoicing in God's goodness,
              that God is Who is,
    and in desiring God's honor and glory.

These acts should be made
    insofar as is possible for they are
        great awakeners of the will.

When the Lord gives them these acts,
    such souls would be well advised
        not to abandon them
    to finish the usual meditation.

LOVE

The important thing is not to think much,
but to love much,
and so do that which best
stirs you to love.

Perhaps we don't know what love is.
I wouldn't be surprised.

It doesn't consist in great delight,
but in desiring strong determination
to please God in everything,
in striving, insofar as possible,
not to offend God
and in asking God
for the advancement of the
honor and glory of God's Son
and the increase of the Catholic Church.

These are the signs of Love.

SELF KNOWLEDGE

Oh Lord, take into account
the things we suffer on this path
for lack of knowledge.

The trouble is
>that since we do not think there is
>anything to know other than that we must
>>think of you,
>we do not even know
>>how to ask those whom we know,
>nor do we understand
>>what there is to ask.

We suffer terrible trials
>because we don't understand ourselves,
>and that which isn't bad at all,
>but good, we think is a serious fault.

INTERIOR WORLD WITHIN

People don't stop to reflect
>that there is an interior world within us.

For all this turmoil in my head doesn't
>hinder prayer or what I am saying,
>but the soul is completely taken up in
>>its quiet, love, desires,
>>>>and clear knowledge.

The experiences that I call
>spiritual delight in God, that I termed
>>elsewhere the prayer of quiet,
>are of a very different kind
>>as those of you will know
>>>if you have experienced them
>>>>by the mercy of God.

FOUNTAINS OF WATER

For a better understanding, let's consider
    that we see two founts
        with two water troughs.

I don't find anything more appropriate
    to explain some spiritual experiences
        than water.
    This may be because I know little
    and have no helpful cleverness of mind.

I am so fond of this element
    that I have observed it more attentively
    than many other things.

In all things
    so great and wise a God has created
        there must be many beneficial secrets.

Those who understand them do benefit, although
    I believe that in each little thing
        created by God
    there is more than what is understood,
        even if it is a little ant.

TROUGHS

These two troughs are filled with water in
        many different ways;
with one, water comes from far away
        through many aqueducts and the use
                of much ingenuity;
with the other,
        the source of water is right there,
                and the trough fills without any noise.

If the spring is abundant,
    as is this one we are speaking about,
        the water overflows
                once the trough is filled
                        forging a large stream.

There is no need of any skill,
        nor does the building of aqueducts
                have to continue,
                        but the water is always flowing
                                from the spring.

AQUEDUCTS

The water coming from the aqueducts
    is comparable to the consolations
    that are drawn from meditation.

For we obtain them through thoughts,
    assisting ourselves,
        using creatures to help our meditation,
        and tiring the intellect.

In the end, the consolation
    comes through our own efforts.
Noise is made when there has to be some
    replenishing of the benefits
    the consolation causes in the soul.

SPRING

With this other fount,
    the water comes from its own source,
            God.

And, since God desires to do so,
    God produces this delight
    with the greatest peace
        and quiet and sweetness
in the very interior part of ourselves.

I don't know from where or how,
nor do I know if such happiness and
    delight experienced are
        earthly consolations in the heart.

There is no similarity at the beginning,
for afterward the delight fills everything;
    this water overflows through
    all the dwelling places and faculties
        until reaching the body.

That is why I said
    that it begins in God
        and ends in ourselves.

Certainly the whole exterior person
            enjoys this
    spiritual delight and sweetness.

CRUCIBLE OF PRAYER

It seems clear to me
  that in some way we must unite
    our wills with God's will.

But it is in the effects and
  deeds following afterwards
      that one discerns the true
        value of prayer.

There is no better crucible for
    testing prayer than compassion.

SHEPHERD'S WHISTLE

Once the great King,
    who is in the center dwelling place,
    sees the good will of those
    who walk in the environs of the castle,
    He desires, in His mercy,
    to bring them back to Him.

Like a good shepherd,
    with a whistle so gentle that even they
    themselves almost fail to hear it,
He makes them recognize His voice
    and brings them back to their
    dwelling place.

And this shepherd's whistle has such power
    that they abandon the exterior things
    in which they were estranged from Him
    and enter the castle.

When God grants the favor,
    it is a great help to seek God within,
    where God is found more easily
    and in a way more beneficial to us
    than when sought through one's own effort.

LISTENING IN LOVE

Don't think this recollection is acquired
    by the intellect striving to think
    about God within itself.
This method is good
    and an excellent kind of meditation
        because it is founded on a truth,
            which is that God is within us.

But this isn't the prayer of recollection
    because it is something each one can do.

Sometimes
    before people begin to think
        of God,
    they find that they are already
        inside the castle.

I don't know
    in what way
        or how they heard
            their Shepherd's whistle.

It wasn't through their ears
    because nothing is heard.

But one noticeably senses a
    gentle drawing inward.

And this recollection
   is a preparation for
      being able to listen,
         so that the soul,
instead of striving to engage in discourse,
   strives to remain attentive and aware
   of what the Lord is working in it.

WAKE UP

To journey into this
   interior world within,
   love must already be awakened.

For love to awaken in us:

      Let Go, Let Be,
      Be Silent
      Be Still in Gentle Peace,
      Be Aware of Opposites,
   Learn Mindfulness and Forgetfulness.

LET GO, LET BE

First, in this work of the Spirit,
the one who thinks less
and has less desire to act
does more.

What we must do is to beg
like the needy poor
before a rich and great emperor,
and then lower our eyes
and wait with humility.

BE SILENT

When through God's secret paths it seems
　　that we understood that God hears us,
　　　then it is good to be silent.

Since God allowed us to remain near God,
　　it will not be wrong to avoid working
　　　with the intellect.
But if we don't know yet whether
　　the King has heard or seen us,
　　　　we mustn't become fools.

The soul does become quite a fool
　　when it tries to induce this prayer.
　　　It is left much drier and the
　　　　imagination becomes more restless.

The Lord desires that we beseech God and
　　call to mind that we are in God's presence.
God knows what is suitable for us.

What God did not reserve are many
　　　other efforts we can make with God's help;
　　　such as prayer and penance,
　　　　good deeds and suffering.

BE STILL IN GENTLE PEACE

The second reason is that
    these interior works are all
        gentle and peaceful;
doing something arduous would cause
        more harm than good.

Leave the soul in God's hands.
Let God do whatever God wants with it,
    with the greatest disinterest as possible
        about your own benefits
           and
the greatest resignation to the will of God.

BE AWARE OF OPPOSITES

The fourth reason
is that the very care
used not to think of anything
will perhaps rouse the mind
to think of everything.

LEARN MINDFULNESS AND FORGETFULNESS

The fifth and what is most essential
and pleasing to God is that we be
mindful of God's honor and glory
and forget ourselves
and our own profit
and comfort and delight.

EXPANSION

What an expansion the soul is !
This may be clearly understood using the
fount as an example.

The fount
doesn't overflow into a stream.
It is constructed of such material
that the more water there is
flowing into it,
the larger the trough becomes.

So it seems is the case with this prayer
and with many other marvels
God grants to the soul.

God enables and prepares it
so that it can keep
everything within itself.

This interior sweetness and expansion
can be verified in the fact
that the soul
is not as tied down as it was before.

It has much more freedom.

SUCKLING CHILD

In this prayer the soul is not yet grown
      but is like a suckling child.

When the child turns away
      from the mother's breasts,
      what can be expected from it but death?

I am very much afraid that this will happen
      to anyone to whom God has granted
      this favor and who withdraws from prayer,
      unless it is done for a particularly
      special reason.

If one does not return quickly to prayer,
      things will go from bad to worse.

Path III: Transforming Energy

© 1984 Clairvaux, osf.

"*The silkworm begins to spin the silk and build the house wherein it will die. This house is Christ.*"

TREASURE

Few of us dispose ourselves
    that the Lord may communicate
        this treasure,
    this pearl of contemplation to us.

In exterior matters we are proceeding well
so that we will reach what is necessary.

But in the practice of the virtues
that are necessary for arriving
        at this point
we need very, very much,
        we cannot be careless
    in either small things or great.

Be brave in begging the Lord
    to give us his grace in such a way
    that nothing will be lacking
        through our own fault;

That he will show us the way
    and will so strengthen the soul
    that it will dig until it finds the
        hidden treasure.

The truth is that the treasure
    lives within our very selves.

NO CLINGING—LET GO

The Lord doesn't want you
　　to hold on to anything,
　　　　for if you avoid doing so,
you will be able to enjoy the favors
　　we are speaking of.

Whether you have little or much,
　　the Lord wants everything;
and in conformity with what you know
　　　　you have given,
you will receive greater or lesser favors.

WINE CELLAR

Now recall what you have heard
    the bride say in the Song of Songs:

      "He brought me into the wine cellar."

I understand this union
        to be the wine cellar
    where the Lord wishes to place us
      when he desires and as he desires.

But however great the effort we make
    to do so, we cannot enter.
The Lord must place us there
  and enter himself
      into the center of our soul.

He wants to enter the center of the soul
    without going through any door as he
    entered the place where his disciples were
    when he said,
      "Pax vobis,"
  or as he left the tomb without
      lifting away the stone.

THE PROCESS: CREATION

You have already heard about God's marvels
manifested in the way silk originates,
for only God could have invented something
like that.

The silkworms come from seeds
about the size of little grains of pepper.

When the warm weather comes
and the leaves begin to appear
on the mulberry tree,
the seeds start to live,
for they are dead until then.

The worms nourish themselves
on the mulberry leaves
until, having grown to full size,
they settle on some twigs.

There, with their little mouths,
they themselves go
about spinning the silk
and making some very thick little cocoons
in which they enclose themselves.

The silkworm, which is fat and ugly, then dies,
and a little white butterfly, very pretty,
comes forth from the cocoon.

LETTING GO

The silkworm starts to live
by the heat of the Holy Spirit.
When it begins to benefit
through general help given to us all by God
and through remedies left
by God to the church,
by going to confession,
by reading good books, and
by hearing sermons.

These are the remedies
that a soul
can make use of
when it becomes dead in its carelessness
and placed in the midst of
harmful situations.

It begins to live
and to sustain itself by these things
and by good meditations until it is grown.

When this silkworm is grown,
it begins to spin the silk
and build the house
wherein it will die.

This house is Christ.

LETTING BE

Let us be quick to do this work and
    weave this little cocoon by taking away
    our self-love,
        our self-will,
        our clinging to any earthly thing;
        by performing deeds of penance,
        prayer, mortification, obedience
        and all the other things you know.

Let it die;
let this silkworm die
    as it does in completing
   what it was created to do.

And you will see
          how we see God,
      as well as ourselves,
    placed inside God's grandeur
     in this little silkworm
      within its cocoon.

BREAKTHROUGH

Oh, now, though it has never been
      quieter and calmer in its life,
To see the restlessness
      of this little butterfly
            is something to praise God for!

The difficulty is
that it doesn't know
      where to alight and rest.

Since it has experienced such wonderful rest,
      all that it sees on earth displeases it,
especially if God gives it this wine often.
      Almost each time it gains new treasures.

It no longer has any esteem
   for the works it did while a worm.
 Leaving the cocoon,
      little by little
            it now has wings.

How can it be happy
walking step by step
      when it can fly?

LOSE LIFE TO FIND LIFE

What reasonings could make us conclude
      that a thing as non-rational
         as a worm or a bee
could be so diligent in working
      for our benefit
         and with so much industriousness?

And the poor little worm
      loses its life in the challenge.

This is enough for a period of meditation
      even though I may say no more to you.

In it you can consider
      the wonders and the wisdom of our God.

We can see what we can do
      with the help of God.
God Herself,
         as She does in this prayer of union,
         becomes
the dwelling place we build for ourselves.

It seems I am saying
   that we can build up God
          and take God away,
  since I say
    that God is the dwelling place
    and we ourselves can build it
      so as to place ourselves in it.
     And, indeed we can!

Not that we can take God away

        or build God up.

But, we can take away
   from ourselves
     and build up
        as do these little silkworms.

TRANSFORMATION

When the soul is in this prayer,
truly dead to the world,
a little white butterfly comes forth.

O greatness of God!

How transformed the soul is
when it comes out of the prayer
after having been placed within the
greatness of God,

and so closely joined with God
for a little while.

SHADOW

Oh, Lord,
    what new trials begin for this soul!

Who would say such a thing
after a favor so sublime?
I don't mean to say
    that those who arrive here
        do not have peace;
        they do have it, and it is very deep.

For the trials themselves are so valuable
        and have such roots
            that although very severe
they give rise to peace and happiness.

Oh, greatness of God!
    A few years ago—and perhaps days—
                    the soul
wasn't mindful of anything but itself.

Who has placed it
        in the midst of such painful concerns?

WAX AND SEAL

Indeed the soul does no more in this union
　　than does wax when another
　　　　impresses a seal on it.

The wax doesn't impress the seal upon itself;
　　it is only disposed of by being soft.

And even in order to be disposed,
　　it doesn't soften itself
　　　　but remains still
　　　　　　and gives its consent.

O, goodness of God
　　everything must be at a cost to you!

All you want is our will
　　and that there be no impurity in the wax.

COMPASSION

Let us now get back to our little dove,
    and see something about what gives it
    in this state.

It must always be understood
    that one has to strive to go forward
      in the service of the Lord
        and in self·knowledge.

For it gives forth the seed
    that produces other silkworms,
      and its self dies forever.

I say that it "gives forth the seed"
    because I hold that it is God's desire
    that a favor so great not be given in vain,
      but that it be for benefit of others.

Left with these desires and virtues,
    the soul always brings profit
      to other souls
    during the time that it continues
      to live virtuously;
    and they catch fire from its fire.

You must note that there are
different kinds of sufferings.

Some sufferings are produced suddenly
by our human nature,
and the same goes
for consolation,
and even by the charity of
compassion for one's neighbor,
as our Lord experienced
when he raised Lazarus.

LACK OF LOVE

Alas for us,
    how few there must be
        who reach this union,
    although whoever guards oneself
        against offending the Lord,
    and has lived a prayerful style of life
        thinks that everything has been done.

Oh, but there remain some worms,
    unrecognized until,
like those in the story of Jonah
    which gnawed away the ivy,
        they have gnawed the virtues.

This happens through
    self-love, self-esteem,
        judging one's neighbors;
even though in little things,
    a lack of charity for them,
        and not loving them
        as ourselves.

Even though, while crawling along,
    we fulfill our obligation
        and no sin is committed,
we don't advance very far
    in what is required
        for complete union
           with the will of God.

LOVE OF NEIGHBOR, LOVE OF GOD

The Lord asks two things:
Love of God
and
love of neighbor.

This is what we must work for.

The most certain sign as to whether
we are observing these two laws
is whether we observe well the
love of neighbor.

Although there are strong indications
for recognizing that we do love God,
we cannot truly know whether or not this
is so, but we can know whether we
love our neighbor.

And be certain that
the more advanced you see you are
in love for your neighbor,
the more certain you will be
in the love of God,
for the love God has for us
is so great that to repay us for our
love of neighbor,
God will, in a thousand ways,
increase our love of God.

I cannot doubt this.

ATTENTIVENESS

It is important for us
 to walk with careful attention
  to how we are proceeding
   in this matter,
for if we practice love of neighbor
  with great perfection,
   we will have done everything.

We will not reach perfection
 in the love of neighbor
  if that love doesn't rise
from the love of God at its roots.

JUDGE BY DEEDS

Since this is so important to us,
    let us try to understand ourselves
        even in little things,
and pay no attention to any big plans
      that sometimes suddenly come to us
        during prayer, in which it seems
          we will do wonders for our neighbor,
and even for just one soul,
      so that it might be saved.

If afterward our deeds
    are not in conformity with those plans,
      there will be no reason to believe
        that we will accomplish the plans.

DESIRES

I am amused sometimes
    to see certain souls
    who think when they are at prayer
that they would like to be humiliated
    and publicly insulted for God,
and afterward they would hide a tiny fault
        if they could;
or, if they have not committed one
    and yet are charged with it—

            God deliver us!

When I see souls very earnest
in trying to understand
        the prayer they have,
            and very sullen when they are in it,
it makes me realize how little they understand
        of the way by which union is attained.

It seems they don't dare
    let their minds move or stir
        lest a bit of their spiritual delight
            and devotion be lost.

COMPASSIONATE WORKS

Is it good feelings that the Lord wants?
No, absolutely not;
works are what the Lord wants.

He desires that if you see a person who is sick
to whom you can bring relief,
you have compassion.

Do not worry about losing your recollection
when you meet someone in need.

What the Lord wants
is for us to suffer with those who suffer;
to fast so that others might eat.

Compassion is what the Lord desires.

LOST

When we fail to love our neighbor we are
lost.

> May it please the Lord
> that this will never be so.

For if you do not fail,
> I tell you that you shall receive from
> God
> the union that God promised.

When you see yourselves lacking in this love,
> even though you have devotion and
> gratifying experiences
> > that make you think you have
> > reached this stage,

and you experience some
> suspension in the prayer of quiet,

believe me,
> you have not reached union.

SPIRITUAL ESPOUSAL

I want to explain more to you about what I
   think this prayer of union is.

You have already heard
   that God espouses souls spiritually.
And even though this comparison may be a
   coarse one, I cannot find another
      that would better explain what I mean
       than the sacrament of marriage.

This spiritual espousal is different in kind
       from marriage;
for in these matters that we are dealing with
   there is never anything
     that is not spiritual.

    For it is all a matter of
      love
    united with love,
  and the actions of love are most pure
  and extremely delicate and gentle,
that there is no way of explaining them,
    but the Lord knows
   how to make them clearly felt.

ENGAGEMENT

It seems to me that
　　this prayer of union
　　　　does not reach
　　　　　　　the stage of spiritual betrothal.

　　Here below when two people are engaged,
　　　　　　there is discussion about
　　　　　whether they are alike,
　　　whether they love each other, and
　　　whether they might meet together
so as to become more satisfied with each other.

So, too, in the case of this union with God,
　　　　　the agreement has been made,
　　and this soul is well informed about the
　　　　　　goodness of her Spouse
　　and determined to do God's will in everything,
　　and in as many ways as she sees, might make
　　　　　　God happy.

　　　　And God,
　　as one who understands clearly
whether these things about the betrothed are so,
　　　　is happy with her.

　　　As a result God grants this mercy,
　　for God desired her to know Him more
　　and that they might meet together,
　　　　　as they say,
　　　　and be united.

ADVANCING

We very often think
    that if God abandons us,
        we will soon end in the abyss.

We should walk with special care and attention,
observing how we are proceeding
        in the practice of virtue,
whether we are getting better or worse in some areas
    especially in love for one another,
        and in the desire
      to be considered least among others
      and in the performance of ordinary tasks.

We strive always to advance in the love of God.
        Love can never be idle.

DARKNESS AND MISUNDERSTANDING

There is a loud outcry by individuals
    with whom one is dealing
        and even by those one does not deal with
and who, it seems, never even think of the person.

An example?

    Gossip like the following:

        "She's trying to make out she's a saint;
        she goes to extremes to deceive the world
            and bring others to ruin;
        there are better Christians
            who don't put on this outward show."

PRAISE

Praise is just another trial.
    Later on, praise is not so intolerable.

First, because experience makes the soul
    see clearly that people are as quick to say
        good things or bad.
So it pays no more attention
    to the good things than to the bad.

Second, because it has been
    more enlightened by the Lord
        that no good thing comes from itself
            but is given by God.
And it turns to praise God,
    forgetful that it had any part to play,
        just as if it had seen the gift
            in another person.

Third, if it sees that some souls have benefitted
    from seeing the favors God grants it,
        it thinks that God
            used this means
    of being falsely esteemed as good,
so that some blessings might come to those souls.

Fourth, since it looks after the
   honor and glory of God
     more than its own,
the fear which came in the beginning,
   that this process will destroy it, is removed;
     little does dishonor matter to it
   if in exchange God might perhaps thereby
     just once be praised.

Afterwards, let whatever comes come.

   After letting go, one must let be.

LIVING WITH PRAISE AND BLAME

And when the soul reaches the stage
    at which it pays little attention to praise,
it pays much less to disapproval;
    on the contrary, it rejoices in this
        and finds it a very sweet truth.
           This is an amazing truth.

        Blame does not intimidate the soul,
           but strengthens it.
    Experience has already taught it
the wonderful gain that comes on this path.

Other sufferings and illnesses
    of many kinds are the usual thing.
I would always choose the path of suffering,
    if only to imitate our Lord Jesus Christ
    if there were no other gains,
especially since there are always so many
        other things to gain.

WAITING FOR NEW BIRTH

There is no remedy in this tempest of
        darkness and confusion but to wait
        for the mercy of God.
For at an unexpected time,
        with one word alone or a chance happening,
God so quickly calms the soul
            that it seems that there had not been
                even as much as a cloud in that soul,
            and it remains filled with sunlight
                and much more consolation.

In this state of darkness
        grace is so hidden,
            that not even a tiny spark is visible.

These experiences are indescribable,
        for they are spiritual affections
        and sufferings
            and one doesn't know
                what to call them.

WORKS OF CHARITY

The best remedy

is to engage

in external works of charity

and to hope

in the mercy of God

Who never fails those who hope in Her.

May God be forever blessed.

Amen.

DELIGHTFUL. WOUND OF LOVE

The soul feels that it is wounded
   in the most delightful way,
      but it doesn't know
         how or by whom
            it was wounded.

It knows clearly
   that the wound is something precious
   and it would never want to be cured.

It complains to its spouse
   with words of love,
      even outwardly,
         without being able to do otherwise,
           and the pain is great,
              although delightful and sweet.

The wound satisfies it much more
   than the delightful and painless absorption
      of the prayer of quiet.

ENKINDLINGS FROM THE SPARK OF GOD

It's as though from this fire
   enkindled in the brazier that is my God
      a spark leaps forth
and so strikes the soul
   that the flaming fire is felt by it.

And since the spark is not enough
     to set the soul on fire,
and the fire is so delightful,
   the soul is left with that pain;
     but the spark
       merely by touching the soul
       produces that effect.

This is the best comparison I have found.

This pain is never permanent.

For this reason it doesn't set the soul on fire,
but just as the fire is about to start,
the spark goes out and the soul is left
with the desire to suffer again
that loving pain
the spark causes.

Let the one to whom our Lord
has granted this favor
fear that he might prove ungrateful
for so generous a favor,
and strive to better his entire life,
and to serve.
The results will be to receive more and more.

LOCUTIONS—WORDS OF LOVE

God has another way of awakening the soul.
God speaks within one's being.

There are many kinds of locutions,
words of love,
given to the soul.

Some seem to come from outside oneself;
others from deep within.
And, some are so exterior
that they come through a sense of hearing,
for it seems there is a spoken word.

Such words can be from God
or from the devil
as from one's own imagination.

SIGNS OF GOD'S GIFTS

The surest signs that they are from God
    that can be had are these:

The first and truest
    is the power and authority they bear,
      for words of love from God
        affect what they say.

    A soul finds itself in the midst of all
      the tribulations and disturbances,
        in darkness of the intellect
          and in dryness.
      With one word alone of these
        that the Lord says,
        "Don't be distressed,"
it is left calm and free from all distress,
      with great light and
      without all suffering.

    Or a soul is afflicted with fear
      and with one word alone,
        "It is I, fear not,"
    the fear is taken away completely
    and the soul is most comforted.

    Or it is greatly distressed
over how certain business matters
      will turn out;
    it hears that it should be calm
and everything will turn out all right.
It is left certain and free of anxiety.

The second sign
    is the great quiet life in the soul,
        the devout and peaceful recollection,
      the readiness to engage
        in the praise of God.

The third sign is that
    these words remain in the memory
      for a very long time,
   and, some are never forgotten
      as are those we listen to here on earth.
If these signs are present,
  there can be a great deal of certainty
     that the words of love are from God.

If the words come
  from the imagination,
     there are none of these signs.

      Neither certitude,
         nor interior peace
     nor interior delight.

TREASURE CHAMBER

You enter into the room of a king
        or a great lord,
                or, I believe, they call it
                        the treasure chamber,
        where there are countless kinds
                of glass and earthen vessels
                and other things so arranged
                        that upon entering
                the soul sees almost all these objects.

The soul, while it is made one with God,
        is placed in this room of treasures
                that we must have interiorly.
After it returns to itself
        the soul is left with the representation
                of the grandeurs it saw,
        but it cannot describe any of them.

In a rapture, God carries off
        the entire soul, and, as to someone who is
                God's spouse,
        begins showing it some little part
        of the kingdom it has gained
                by being espoused to God.

STRAW AND EMBER

It seems that the soul is so often,
  so earnestly, and so completely willing
  to offer everything to God.

The soul should understand that in itself
    it has no longer any part to play.
Also, it is carried off with a noticeably
    more impetuous movement.

It is determined now to do no more
than what the straw does
  when drawn by an ember
    —if you have noticed—
and abandon itself into the hands of the One
      who is all powerful,
for it sees that the safest thing to do
  is to make a virtue of necessity.

And that I mentioned a straw
    is certainly appropriate,
    for as easily as a tall giant
      snatches a straw,
        this great and powerful giant
        carries away the spirit.

WAVES AND THE BARK

It seems that the trough of water within
  filled so easily and gently.

Here the great God,
      who holds back the springs of water
          and doesn't allow the sea
          to go beyond its boundaries,
              lets loose the springs
  from which the water in this trough flows.

With a powerful impulse,
      a huge wave rises up so forcefully
          that it lifts high this little bark
              that is our soul.

A bark cannot prevent the furious waves
      from leaving it where they will;
          nor does the pilot have the power,
          nor do those who take part
              in controlling the ship.

INSIGHT

It happens that within an instant
    so many things together are taught
        that, if one were to work for many years
            with the imagination and mind
            in order to systematize them
                one wouldn't be able to do so,
    not with even one thousandth of them.

SUN AND ITS RAYS

        I have often thought
        that just as the sun while in the sky
            has such strong rays,
    that, even though it doesn't move from there,
        the rays promptly reach the earth,
            so the soul and the spirit,
                which are one,
        could be like the sun and its rays.

JEWELS FROM THE CREATOR

These are the jewels the Spouse begins
to give the betrothed:

Knowledge of the grandeur of God
and greater understanding;
Self‑knowledge and humility
in realizing God's gifts;

Letting go of things in order to be
of greater service to God.

ENERGY OF LOVE

This little butterfly is unable
    to find a lasting place of rest;
rather, since the soul goes about
    with such tender love,
any occasion that enkindles this fire more
    makes the soul fly aloft.

It would want to enter
    into the midst of the world
        to try to play a part in getting
            even one soul
                to praise God more.

A woman in this stage of prayer is distressed
        by the natural hindrance there is
            to her entering the world,
and she envies those who have the freedom
        to cry out and to spread the news abroad
            about who this great God of Hosts is.

GIFT OF TEARS

Let us not think that everything
    is accomplished through much weeping
      but set our hands
      to the task of hard work and virtue.
These are what we must pay attention to.

Let the tears come when God sends them
    and without any effort
        on our part to induce them.

The tears from God will irrigate this dry earth,
    and they are a great help in producing fruit.
The less attention we pay to them,
    the more there are,
      for they are the water
        that flows from heaven.

The tears we draw out by tiring ourselves
    in digging cannot compare
      with the tears that come from God.
For often in digging
    we shall get worn out
      and not find even a puddle of water,
        much less a flowing well.

THE GOOD GUIDE—JESUS

It will also seem to you
   that anyone who enjoys such lofty things
   will no longer meditate on the mysteries
     of the most sacred humanity
     of our Lord Jesus Christ.
Such a person
   would now be engaged entirely in loving.

I cannot imagine what such souls are thinking.

To be always withdrawn
   from bodily things and enkindled in love
   is the trait of angelic spirits,
     not of those who live in mortal bodies.

It's necessary that we speak to,
   think about,
     and become the companions of those who,
       having had a mortal body,
     accomplished such great feats for God.

How much more is it necessary
     not to withdraw through one's own efforts
     from all our good and help,
       which is the most sacred humanity
         of our Lord Jesus Christ.

For if they lose the Guide,
who is the good Jesus,
they will not hit on the right road.

It will be quite an accomplishment
if they remain safely
in the other dwelling places.

The Lord himself says
that he is the Way,
that he is the Light
and that no one can go to the Father
but through him,
and "anyone who sees me sees my father."

CHANGES IN PRAYER

Those whom God has brought to supernatural things
     and to perfect contemplation
     cannot practice discursive reflection.
By meditation
     I mean discursive reflection
     with the intellect in the following way:

          We begin to think about the favor
          God granted us in giving us
               His only son,
          and we do not stop there,
          but go on to the mysteries of his
               whole glorious life;

          or we begin to think about the prayer
               in the garden,
          but the intellect doesn't stop until he
               is on the cross;

          like, let us say, the arrest,
          and we proceed with this mystery
               considering in detail
          the things there are to think of
               and feel about the betrayal of Judas,
          the flight of the apostles,
               and all the rest.

LOVING SPARKS

But a person will not be right
    without dwelling on these mysteries
      or often having them in mind.

Nor is it possible for the soul to forget
    that it has received so much from God,
      so many precious signs of love,
        for these are living sparks
          that will enkindle it more
          in its love for our Lord.

TIME FOR EVERYTHING

Life is long.
In its many trials we need
    to look at Christ, our model,
        how he suffered in his life.
We need to look at his apostles and the saints
        that we may bear our trials with perfection.

Jesus is too good a companion
    for us to turn away from him
        and his most blessed mother,
and he is very pleased
        that we grieve over his sufferings,
        even though we sometimes leave aside
        our own consolation and delight.

Moreover, enjoyment in prayer
        is not so habitual that there is not time
            for everything.

The mistake one can make
        consists not so much of delighting
        in the thought of our Lord Jesus Christ
            but in going along in that absorption,
                waiting for that enjoyment.

JESUS: THE GREAT REMINDER

Although some persons can put many fears
   in those who receive this gift of Jesus' presence,
   they are frequently unable to doubt,
   as in one case, when the Lord said:
     "Do not be afraid, it is I."

These words had so much power that from then on
   there was no doubt about the vision.

Strength and happiness remain
   over such good company.

     The feeling remains
       that God is on the journey, too.

TENDER LOVE AND SERVICE

This continual companionship gives rise
   to a more tender love for God.

   The greatest desire is to surrender
   oneself totally to God's service.

   There is a greater purity of conscience
   because the Presence at its side
makes the soul pay attention to everything.

VESSEL AND STONE

Let us consider how the Lord is present.
It is as though we had in a gold vessel
a precious stone
having the highest value and curative powers.

We know very certainly that it is there
although we have never seen it.
But the powers of the stone do not cease
to benefit us provided that we carry it with us.

Although we have never seen this stone,
we do not on that account cease to prize it,
because through experience we have seen
that it has cured us of some illnesses
for which it is suited.

But we dare not look at it
or open the treasure chest,
nor can we,
because the manner of opening this treasure chest
is known solely
by the one to whom the jewel belongs.

Even though God loaned us the jewel
for our own benefit,
God has kept the key to the treasure chest
and will open it
when God desires to show us the contents.

SUDDEN GIFT AND PEACE

While the soul is very far from thinking
    that anything will be seen, or
    having the thought even pass through its
    mind, a vision is represented to it all at
    once.

The faculties and senses are stirred
    with a great fear and tumult
        so as to place these afterwards
            in a happy place.

Just as there was a tempest and tumult
    that came from heaven
        when St. Paul was hurled to the ground,
here in this interior world
    there is a great stirring;
and in a moment all remains calm,
        and this soul is left so well instructed
        about so many great truths
            it has no need of any teacher.

LEAVE THE PATH TO THE LORD

Although this path may seem very good,
    one to be highly esteemed and revered,
        desiring it is inappropriate.

Believe me, the safest way,
    is to want only what God wants.
God knows more than we ourselves do,
    and God loves us.
Let us place ourselves in God's hands
    so that God's will may be done in us.

It is true that those desires
  to do the will of God
    are supernatural
      and are characteristics of souls
        very much inflamed in love.
Such souls would want the Lord
    to see that they do not serve for pay.
Thus, they never,
as a motion for making the effort to serve more,
think about receiving glory for anything they do.

But their desire is to satisfy love
    and it is love's nature
      to serve with deeds in a thousand ways.

PARDON WRONGS

When will we imitate this great God?
We should very eagerly endure everything.
Let us love the ones
who offend us
since this great God has not ceased
to love us
even though we have offended God very much.
Thus the Lord is right
in wanting us to pardon the wrongs done to us.

TRUTH FROM THE CENTER

God is everlasting truth.

I am reminded of Pilate,
    how he was questioning our Lord
    when during the Passion he asked him,

        "What is truth?"

        and of the little we understand
    about this Supreme Truth.

Let us conclude that in order to live
    in conformity with our God and spouse,
    it will be well if we always study diligently
        how to walk in this truth.

Especially, there should be no desire
    that others consider us
    better than we are.
And in our works
    we should attribute to God
        what is God's
            and to ourselves
                what is ours
and strive to draw out the truth in everything.

WALKING IN TRUTH

Once I was pondering why our Lord
was so fond of this
        virtue of humility,
and this thought came to me
not as a result of reflection
        but suddenly.

It is because God is supreme Truth;
    and to be humble
    is to walk in truth,
for it is a very deep truth
        that of ourselves we have nothing good
            but only emptiness
                and nothingness.

Whoever does not understand this
        walks in falsehood.
The more anyone understands it,
        the more this pleases the supreme Truth
            because the person is walking in truth.

        Please God,
    we will be granted the favor
never to leave this path of self-knowledge.

THE BUTTERFLY IS MORE RESTLESS

Do you think that all these favors
the Spouse has bestowed on the soul
will be sufficient to satisfy
the little dove or butterfly
so that it may come to rest
where it will die?

No, certainly not!

Rather this little butterfly is much worse.

Path IV: Union, Ecstasy, Compassion

© 1984 Clairvaux, osf

"Letting go proceeds from the center of the soul and awakens the person to a new consciousness and a new compassion."

VISIT TO THE CENTER

When God is pleased
    to have pity on this soul
    which has already been taken spiritually
        as spouse, because of what it desires,
God brings it,
    before the spiritual marriage is consummated,
    into the seventh dwelling place.

For just as in heaven,
    so in the soul,
        God must have a room
            where God dwells alone.

It's very important for us not to think
    the soul is something dark.
Each one of us has a soul,
    but, since we do not prize souls
        as is deserved by creatures
            made in the image of God,
we do not understand
    the deep secrets that lie in them.

We are not reflecting about something
    restricted to a corner,
    but about an interior world
        where there is room for so many
        and such attractive dwelling places
            as you have seen.

Indeed it is right
   that the soul be like this
      since without it
         there is no dwelling place
            for God.

When God is pleased to grant a soul
      this divine marriage,
God first brings the soul
   into God's own dwelling place.
God desires that the favor be different
   from what it was at other times
      when God gave the soul raptures.

But it doesn't seem to the soul
   that it is called to enter its center,
      as it is here in this dwelling place,
   but called to the deeper regions within.

CLOUD OF SPLENDOR

In this seventh dwelling place
the union comes about in a different way:
 Our good God now desires
 to remove the scales from the soul's eye
 and let it see and understand
 something of the favor God grants it.

When the soul is brought
 into that dwelling place,
 the most blessed Trinity
 is revealed to it
 through a certain representation of truth
 —an intellectual vision.

First, there comes an enkindling in the spirit
 in the manner of a cloud
 of magnificent splendor.
 These Persons are distinct;
 and, through an admirable knowledge,
the soul understands as a most profound truth
 that all three Persons are one substance,
 and one Power,
 and one Knowledge
 and one God alone.

Here all three Persons communicate
themselves to it,
speak to it,
and explain those words of the Lord
in the Gospel,
that he
and the Father
and the Holy Spirit
will come to dwell with the soul
that loves God
and keeps God's commandments.

OCCUPIED IN THE SERVICE OF THE LORD

You may think that as a result
    the soul will be outside of itself
        and so absorbed that it will be unable
            to be occupied with anything else.

On the contrary,
    the soul is much more occupied than before
with everything pertaining to the service of God,
    and once its duties are over
        it remains with that enjoyable company.

MARRIAGE

Now let us deal
          with the divine and spiritual marriage,
although this great favor
     does not come to its fullness,
          as long as we live.
For if we were to withdraw from God,
     this remarkable blessing would be lost.

In the spiritual marriage
     there is still much less remembrance
          of the body
because this secret union takes place
     in the very interior center of the soul,
          which must be where God is.
There is no need of any door for God to enter.

This is because everything
     that has been said up until now
     seems to take place
     by means of the senses and faculties,
and this appearance
     of the humanity of the Lord must also.
But that which comes to pass
in the union of the spiritual marriage
     is very different.
The Lord appears in the center of the soul,
     not in an imaginative vision,
          but in an intellectual one,
     although more delicate than those mentioned,
               as he appeared to the apostles
               without entering through the door
when he said to them "Peace be with you."

MADE ONE WITH GOD

What God communicates here to the soul,
    in an instant,
      is a secret so great
      and a favor so sublime—
and the delight the soul experiences
    so extreme,
      that I don't know what to compare it to.

One can say no more
    than the spirit is made one with God.
God has desired to be so joined with the creature.
    Just as those who are married
      cannot be separated,
God doesn't want to be separated from the soul.

The spiritual betrothal is different,
    for the two often separate.
And the union is also different because,
    even though it is the
    joining of two things into one,
      in the end the two can be separated
      and each remains by itself.

In this favor of the Lord, this is not so.

WAX AND CANDLES,
RAIN INTO THE RIVER,
WINDOW AND LIGHT

The soul always remains with its God
in that center.

Let us say that the union
is like the joining of two wax candles
to such an extent
that the flame coming from them is but one,
or that the flame and the wax are all one.

But afterward one can be easily separated
from the other
and there are two candles.
The same holds for the wick.

In the spiritual marriage the union is like
what we have when rain falls
from the sky into a river or fount.
All is water,
for the rain that falls from heaven
cannot be divided or separated
from the water of the river.
Or it is like
what we have when a little stream
enters the sea.
There is no means of separating the two.
Or, like the bright light entering a room
through two different windows.

Although the streams of light are separate
when entering the room,
   they become one.

Perhaps this is what St. Paul means in saying,
      "He that is joined or united
         to the Lord
    becomes one spirit with him."

Perhaps, he is referring
to this sovereign marriage,
presupposing that God
has brought the soul through it to union.

And he also says,
       "For me to live in Christ,
        and to die is gain."

The soul can say these words now,
   because this state is the place
     where the little butterfly dies
      and with the greatest joy
    because its life is now in Christ.

BREASTS OF GOD

O Lord of my life.
Sustenance that sustains me.

From those divine breasts
where it seems God is always
sustaining the soul
there flow streams of milk
bringing comfort
to all the people of the castle.

It seems the Lord desires
that in some manner
these others in the castle
may enjoy the great gift
the soul is enjoying.

From that full-flowing river,
where this tiny fount is swallowed up,
a spurt of that water
will sometimes be directed
toward the sustenance of those
who in corporal things
must serve these two who are wed.

Just as a distracted person would feel this water
if he were suddenly bathed in it,
and would be unable to avoid feeling it,
so are these operations recognized
even with greater certitude.

Just as a gush of water
        could not reach us without a source,
            it is understood clearly
        that there is someone in the interior depths
                who shoots these arrows.

Life is given to this life,
        and there is a sun
        in the interior of the soul
        from which a brilliant light proceeds
            and is sent to the faculties.

LETTING GO

It is very certain
   that in emptying ourselves
      of all that is creature
and letting go for the love of God,
       the same Lord will fill us with himself.

When Jesus our Lord
     was once praying for his apostles,
        he said they were one with the Father
          and with him,
           just as Jesus Christ our Lord
          is in the Father
       and the Father is in him.
I just don't know what greater love
   there can be than this.

All of us are included here,
   for God said:
      "I ask not only for them,
        but for all those
         who will also believe in me,"
and
         "I am in them."

All things must come to the soul
   from its roots,
     from where it is planted.
The tree that is beside the running water
   is fresher and gives more fruit.

TRIALS AND PEACE

It should not be thought
   that the faculties,
      senses, and passions
         are always in this peace;
            the soul is, yes.

But in those other dwelling places,
   times of war, trial, and fatigue are never lacking.
However, they are such
   that they do not as a rule
      take the soul from its place of peace.

That there are trials and sufferings
   and that at the same time
      the soul is at peace
         is difficult to explain.

NEW LIFE OF THE BUTTERFLY

This little butterfly has already died,
   with supreme happiness
      for having found repose
         and that Christ lives in it.

Let us see what kind of life it lives,
   or how this life differs
      from the life it was living.

STRANGE FORGETFULNESS

The first effect
    is a forgetfulness of self,
      for truly the soul
          seemingly no longer is.

        The soul experiences
      a strange forgetfulness
       for it no longer is
      or would want to be
      anything in anything
    except when it understands
   that there can come from itself
something by which the glory and honor of God
    may increase even one degree.

For this purpose the soul
    would very willingly lay down its life.
For no earthly thing would it fail to do
    all it can in the service of our Lord.

LOVE FOR PERSECUTION

The second effect is that the soul
    has a great desire to suffer,
        but not that kind of desire
      that disturbs it as previously.

With much more peace than that mentioned
    and without any hostile feelings
    toward those who do harm,
or any desire to do evil,
    these souls have a deep interior joy
      when persecuted.

Such a soul gains a particular love
    for its persecutors,
      in such a way
that if it sees these in some trial,
    it feels compassion
      and would take on any burden
        to free them from their trial.

The soul eagerly recommends them to God
    and will rejoice to lose the favors
      God grants
if God would bestow
    these same gifts on those others.
Then they will not offend God.

LETTING GO OF EVERYTHING

What surprises me most of all now
    is the great desire to serve the Lord,
    so that the Lord can be praised
    and some soul can benefit.

The glory of one who journeys this far
    is in being able
        in some way
            to help the crucified,
    especially when he so offended.

There are few who,
    letting go of everything else,
    really look after his honor.

There is a great letting go of everything
    and a desire to be always alone
    or occupied in something
        that will benefit some soul.
There are no interior trials
    or feelings of dryness,
but the soul loves with a remembrance
        and tender love of our Lord.

A fire
does not shoot its flame
downward but upward,
no matter how great a fire is enkindled.
Likewise one experiences
that this letting go
proceeds from the center of the soul
and awakens the person to
a new consciousness
and
a new compassion.

NOTE FROM GOD

When this awakening comes to you,
    remember that it comes
    from this interior dwelling place
        where God is in our soul.
                    Praise God very much.

It is like receiving a note or letter from God
    written with intense love.
God wants you alone to understand it.

By no means should you fail to respond
    to God,
        even though you may be extremely occupied
        or in conversation with others.

It is very easy
    since the response is within.
Just try
            "to make an act of love"
or say what St. Paul said,
            "Lord, what will you have me do?"

In many ways God will teach you
    what will be pleasing to God
        and the acceptable time.

REJOICE IN SILENCE AND STILLNESS

In this temple of God,
in this, God's dwelling place,
God alone and the soul
rejoice together in the deepest silence.

When the soul arrives here,
all raptures are taken away.
Perhaps the reason is
that the Lord has now fortified,
enlarged, and made the soul capable.

SYMBOLS OF PEACE AND JOY

These effects,
along with all the other good ones
from the degrees of prayer we mentioned
are given by God when God brings the soul
   to God with this kiss
    sought by the bride.

Here an abundance is given
   to this deer that was wounded.
Here one delights in God's tabernacle.
Here the dove Noah sent out
   to see if the storm was over
    finds the olive branch
     as a sign of firm ground
      discovered amid the floods
       and tempests of this world.

STORMS AND FAIR WEATHER

The cross is not wanting,
   but it doesn't disquiet
      or make one lose peace.

For the storms,
   like a wave,
      pass quickly.

And the fair weather returns,
   because the presence of the Lord
      they experience
         makes them soon forget everything.

WHEN I AM WEAK, THEN I AM POWERFUL

You must not think that these effects
are always present in these souls.
God couldn't grant us a greater favor
than to give us a life
that would be an imitation of the life
God's beloved son lived.

Thus I hold for certain
that these favors
are meant to fortify our weakness,
that we may be able to imitate him
in his great sufferings.

SUFFERING FRIENDS OF THE LORD

We have always seen that those
who were closest to Christ our Lord
    were those with the greatest trials.
Let us look
    not only at what his glorious mother suffered,
        but also the glorious apostles.

How do you think St. Paul could have suffered
    such very great trials?
Through him we can see the
    effect visions and contemplation produce
        when from our Lord
      and not from the imagination
      or the devil's deceit.

Did St. Paul by chance hide himself
    in the enjoyment of these delights
    and not engage in anything else?
You already see
    that he didn't have a day of rest
    from what we can understand,
and neither did he have any rest at night
    since it was then he earned his livelihood.

I like very much the account
    of St. Peter's fleeing from prison
and how our Lord appeared to him and told him,
    "I am on my way to be crucified again."
How did this favor impress St. Peter
    or what did he do?
        He went to straight to his death.

SPIRITUAL MARRIAGE:
BIRTH OF GOOD WORKS

How forgetful this soul
    in which the Lord dwells in so particular
    a way should be of its own rest.
How little it should care for its honor.
How far it should be
    from wanting esteem in anything.
For if it is with God very much,
    it should think little about itself.

All its concern is taken up
    with how to please God more
    and how or where it will show
        the love it bears.

This is the reason for prayer,
    the purpose of the spiritual marriage:
        the birth always of good works.
This is the true sign
    of a favor being from God.

It benefits me little to be alone
    making acts of devotion to our Lord,
        proposing and promising
            to do wonders in service,
if I then go away
    and, when the occasion offers itself,
        do everything the opposite.
I mean it benefits me little in comparison
    with how much greater the benefit is
        when our deeds conform
            with what we say in prayer.

SLAVES OF CHRIST

Keep in mind that I could not exaggerate
       the importance of this.
Fix your eyes on the crucified
    and everything will become small for you.

If God showed love
   by means of such works
       and frightful torments,
how is it you want to please God
       only with words?

Do you know what it means to be truly spiritual?
       It means becoming the slaves of God.

Marked with God's brand,
       which is that of the Cross,
                   spiritual persons,
       because now they have given
           God their liberty,
       can be sold by God as slaves of everyone,
                   as Jesus was.

HUMILITY

This whole building has humility
   as its foundation.

That you might build on good foundations,
   strive to be the least
     and the slaves of all,
   looking at how or where
     you can please and serve them.

It is necessary that your foundation
   consists of more than
     prayer and contemplation.

If you do not strive for the virtues
   and practice this,
      you will always be dwarfs.

WINE FROM THE WINE CELLAR

The soul is fortified
    by the strength it has
        from drinking wine in this wine cellar,
where its God has brought it
    and from where God doesn't allow it to leave,
        and strength flows back to the weak body,
just as food placed in the stomach
    strengthens the head and the whole body.

STRENGTH TO SERVE

This is what I want us to strive for
        and let us desire
                and be occupied in prayer
                        not for the sake of our enjoyment,
                but so as to have this strength to serve.

Let's refuse to take an unfamiliar path,
        for we shall get lost
                at the most opportune time.

It would indeed be novel
        to think of having these favors from God
        through a path other than the one God took
                and the one followed by God's saints.

MARTHA AND MARY—NO DUALISM

Believe me,
   Martha and Mary must join together
      in order to show hospitality to the Lord
        and have him always present
        and not host him badly
     by failing to give him something to eat.

How would Mary, always seated at his feet,
   provide him with food
      if her sister did not help her?

His food nourishes
   so that in every way possible
      we draw souls that may be saved
        and praise him always.

TRUE FRIENDS

People will tell you that you do not
    need friends on this journey,
        that God is enough.

But to be with God's friends is a good way
    to keep close to God in this life.
You will always draw great benefit from them.

This is to love:
    bear with a fault and not be astonished,
    relieve others of their labor and
        take upon yourself tasks to be done;
    be cheerful when others have need of it;
    be grateful for your strength when
        others have need of it;
    show tenderness in love and sympathize
        with the weakness of others.

Friends of God love others far more,
    with a truer, more ardent and
    a more helpful love.
They are always prepared to give much
    more readily than to receive
        even to their Creator.

THE INVITATION

Behold, the Lord invites all.
    Since he is truth itself,
      there is no reason to doubt.

If this invitation were not a general one
    the Lord would not have called us all,
      and even if he called all,
        he wouldn't have promised:
        "I will give you to drink."

        He could have said:
"Come, all of you, for in the end you won't lose
    anything, and to those whom I will choose
      I will give to drink."

But since he spoke without this condition to all,
    I hold as certain that all those who do not
      falter on the way will drink this
        living water.

NO CASTLES IN THE AIR

What I conclude with is
    that we shouldn't build
        castles in the air.

The Lord doesn't look so much
    at the greatness of our works
        as at the love with which they are done.

If you find something good in the way
    I have explained this to you,
        believe that indeed God said it
            so as to make you happy.
        The bad you might find is said by me.

May God our Lord be forever praised and blessed.

        Amen.

BOOKS OF RELATED INTEREST
BY BEAR & COMPANY

THE BOOK OF ANGELUS SILESIUS
by Frederick Franck

HILDEGARD OF BINGEN'S BOOK OF DIVINE WORKS
edited by Matthew Fox

HILDEGARD OF BINGEN'S MEDICINE
by Dr. Wighard Strehlow & Gottfried Hertzka, M.D.

HILDEGARD OF BINGEN'S SCIVIAS
by Hildegard of Bingen, translated by Bruce Hozeski

ILLUMINATIONS OF HILDEGARD OF BINGEN
by Hildegard of Bingen, with commentary by Matthew Fox

MEDITATIONS WITH DANTE ALIGHIERI
by James Collins

MEDITATIONS WITH HILDEGARD OF BINGEN
by Gabriele Uhlein

MEDITATIONS WITH JULIAN OF NORWICH
by Brendan Doyle

MEDITATIONS WITH MECHTILD OF MAGDEBURG
by Sue Woodruff

MEDITATIONS WITH MEISTER ECKHART
by Matthew Fox

MEDITATIONS WITH NICHOLAS OF CUSA
by James Francis Yockey

Contact your local bookseller or write:
BEAR & COMPANY
P.O. Drawer 2860, Santa Fe, NM 87504